The Truth About
UNICORNS

Fireback featuring the royal arms of Great Britain. The unicorn is at right.

The Truth About
UNICORNS

JAMES CROSS GIBLIN

illustrated with drawings by Michael McDermott
and prints and photographs

HarperCollins*Publishers*

The Truth About Unicorns
Text copyright © 1991 by James Cross Giblin
Illustrations copyright © 1991 by Michael McDermott
All rights reserved. No part of this book may be used or reproduced
in any manner whatsoever without written permission except in the
case of brief quotations embodied in critical articles and reviews.
Printed in the United States of America.
For information address HarperCollins Children's Books,
a division of HarperCollins Publishers,
10 East 53rd Street, New York, NY 10022.
Typography by Christine Kettner
2   3   4   5   6   7   8   9   10

Library of Congress Cataloging-in-Publication Data
Giblin, James.
   The truth about unicorns / James Cross Giblin ; illustrated with drawings by
Michael McDermott.
      p.   cm.
   Includes bibliographical references and index.
   Summary: Describes the origins of the unicorn legend, including the real-life
animals that inspired it, and the various myths told about unicorns throughout the world.
   ISBN 0-06-022478-9. — ISBN 0-06-022479-7 (lib. bdg.)
   1. Unicorns — Juvenile literature.   [1. Unicorns.]   I. McDermott,
Michael, ill.   II. title.
GR830.U6G52   1991   90-47233
398.24'54—dc20   CIP
                                                                        AC

DEDICATION

To the two children's librarians—one in Marin County, California,
the other in Lancaster, Pennsylvania—
who asked me at conferences if I'd ever thought of writing
a book about unicorns

Also by James Cross Giblin

THE RIDDLE OF THE ROSETTA STONE:
Key to Ancient Egypt

LET THERE BE LIGHT:
A Book About Windows

FROM HAND TO MOUTH:
Or, How We Invented Knives, Forks, Spoons,
and Chopsticks & the Table Manners
To Go With Them

MILK:
The Fight for Purity

THE TRUTH ABOUT SANTA CLAUS

CHIMNEY SWEEPS:
Yesterday and Today

THE SKYSCRAPER BOOK

Acknowledgments

For their help in providing research material and illustrations, the author thanks the following individuals and institutions:

American Museum of Natural History

The British Tourist Authority

Evans Chan

The Cleveland Museum of Art

Germanisches Nationalmuseum, Nuremberg

Bjarne Kildegaard

Murray Liebman

The Metropolitan Museum of Art

The Museum of Comparative Zoology, Harvard University

The New York Public Library

The Royal Danish Collections at Rosenborg Palace, Copenhagen

Woodfin Camp & Associates

Contents

In a medieval German folk song, a young man stands in a Maytime meadow, enjoying the spring flowers and the songs of birds, when suddenly a horn rings out. Here is what follows:

The hunter stood beside me
　　Who blew that mighty horn;
I saw that he was hunting
　　The gentle unicorn—
But the unicorn is noble,
　　He knows his gentle birth,
He knows that God has chosen him
　　Above all beasts of earth.

The unicorn is noble;
　　He keeps him safe and high
Upon a narrow path and steep
　　Climbing to the sky;
And there no man can take him,
　　He scorns the hunter's dart,
And only a virgin's magic power
　　Shall tame his haughty heart.

The traditional image of the unicorn. Woodcut from The History of Four-Footed Beasts, *1658.*

CHAPTER ONE

A World of Unicorns

AT FIRST GLANCE, the creamy white creature looks very much like a horse. It has the same sort of mane and tail. But then we see the single horn growing out of the animal's forehead, and we know that it is not a horse but a unicorn.

Images of unicorns are all around us today. They can be found on everything from mugs to towels to greeting cards. Sometimes a young girl is shown riding on the unicorn's back as if it were a pet pony. More often the animal stands alone in a sunlit glade, shyly dipping its horn to the ground or raising it proudly toward the heavens.

We've been told—and most of us believe—that no such animal as the unicorn ever lived. Still, its gentle, horselike image is fixed firmly in our minds, and we probably think that is the way the creature has always been pictured. If we do, we're wrong.

Over the centuries, in virtually every corner of the world, people have told and written about many different kinds of unicorns. Some were gigantic, others were tiny and playful. Some had pure white coats, like those we're familiar with, while others had multicolored horns and bodies.

There were unicorns that roared loudly when aroused and unicorns with voices like tinkling bells. Most unicorns fought fiercely and bravely against their enemies, but a few were peaceful animals that never fought anyone.

There was even a real dinosaur unicorn, a large, plant-eating animal whose scientific name is *Monoclonius nasicornus*. It roamed the uplands of northern Asia and North America in the Cretaceous period, about 120 million years ago, though its fossil skeleton was not discovered until this century.

The only thing all these unicorns, real and imaginary, had in common was a single horn on their foreheads. In fact, the word *unicorn*, which comes from the Latin *unicornis*, means "one-horned." But many of the creatures were not

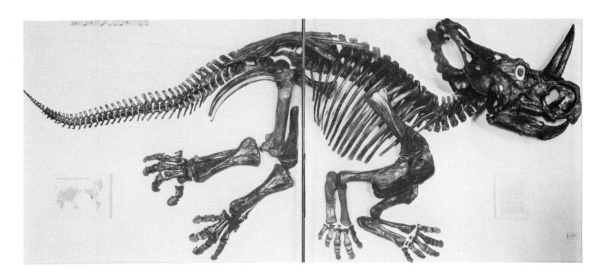

AMERICAN MUSEUM OF NATURAL HISTORY.

Skeleton of Monoclonius, *the dinosaur unicorn.*

called unicorns. They went by that name in Europe and America, but in the Middle East and Far East they were known by other names.

Why, we may wonder, were there so many conflicting notions about the unicorn? Where did people get the idea of a unicorn in the first place? Was it based on any living real animals? And what exactly is it about the unicorn that has fascinated people in all parts of the world for thousands of years and still fascinates us today?

To begin our search for answers to these questions, we need to go back almost 2,500 years and look at the first published description of a unicorn. It was written by a Greek physician named Ctesias (pronounced Tee-see-us) who left his native land in 416 B.C. to accept an appointment from the king of faraway Persia.

CHAPTER TWO

The Beast with
a Three-Colored Horn

IN THE FIFTH CENTURY B.C., the Persian Empire
extended from Turkey in the west to India in the east.
Its capital, Persepolis, was located in what is today Iran.
When Ctesias arrived in Persepolis, he found a bustling
city filled with impressive public buildings. King Darius's
palace, where Ctesias lived and worked, stood atop a
huge limestone terrace, reached by 111 steps.

Caravans from Asia passed constantly through Persepolis, bringing luxury goods made of silk, jade, and ivory
to sell in the city's bazaars. The traders also brought

tales of the wondrous things to be seen in the east, and of the rare and exotic animals that lived there.

Ctesias liked to listen to the traders' tales, and when he returned to Greece in 398 B.C., he wrote a book about his Persian experiences that included many of them. In Ctesias's day, few Greeks traveled beyond the borders of their own country, so there was a large audience for Ctesias's Persian stories. One that made a particularly strong impression was his description of a unicorn.

"There are in India certain wild asses which are as large as horses, and larger," Ctesias wrote. "Their bodies are white, their heads dark red, and their eyes dark blue. They have a horn on the forehead which is about a foot-and-a-half in length. The base of the horn is pure white; the upper part is sharp and a vivid crimson; and the remainder, or middle portion, is black."

As a physician, Ctesias was struck by the medicinal powers the unicorn's horn was said to possess. "Powder filed from this horn is administered in a potion as a protection against deadly poisons," he said, "and if a person drinks water or wine from one of these horns, he will never suffer from convulsions or epilepsy."

Ctesias ended his description of the unicorn with these words: "The animal is exceedingly swift and powerful, so that no creature, neither the horse nor any other, can overtake it."

Ctesias' unicorn.

Ctesias had never been in India and did not claim to have seen a unicorn himself. But no doubt he had heard tales of the fabulous creature from merchants and traders in the bazaars of Persepolis.

Did these merchants really believe there was such an animal as the unicorn? Did Ctesias? The answer is probably yes in both cases. At the time, European knowledge of the world's animals was extremely limited. No one we know of had journeyed to the jungles of Africa and South America, or the vast forests and plains of America, and observed firsthand the animals that were native to those continents. Nor had European travelers explored the remote mountain regions of India. So it's entirely possible that Ctesias believed a wild ass with only one horn lived there.

Actually, Ctesias's unicorn sounds as if it may have been inspired by two other animals that could be found in India. As accounts of these animals were passed on from trader to merchant to people like Ctesias, their traits probably became combined.

One of the animals was most likely a large, fleet-footed antelope that lived in India's Himalaya Mountains. When seen from a distance in profile, the long, straight horns of this antelope often look like a single growth.

The other animal was no doubt the single-horned

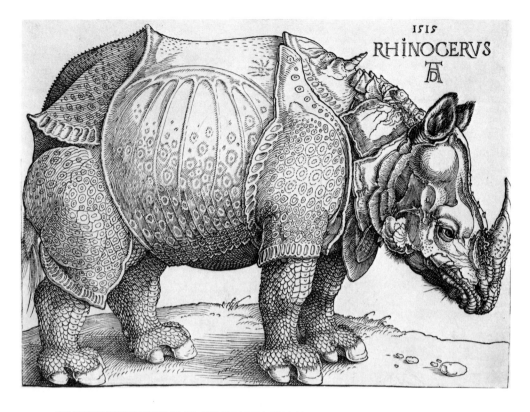

Fanciful drawing of an Indian rhinoceros, based on travelers' tales. Woodcut by Albrecht Dürer (1471–1528).

Indian rhinoceros. Like the unicorn in Ctesias's description, the Indian rhino is a powerful beast that can move quickly despite its great bulk, and outrun most of its enemies.

Contrary to what many people think, the horns of rhinos are not made of bone like the horns of other animals. They are composed instead of keratin, a protein also found in hair and fingernails. The closely compacted keratin that forms a rhino's horn is part of the animal's skin, not its bone structure.

Even so, rhino horn has been prized for its supposed medicinal value since the beginning of history. And, like the unicorn horn described by Ctesias, beakers made of rhino horn were believed to possess healing powers. Indian doctors said that a person who drank from a rhino horn beaker would be protected against poisons, smallpox, and even stomachache. They also claimed that powder from the horn would increase a person's sexual powers.

It's not surprising that the single horns of the Indian rhino and the unicorn were valued so highly. Ancient peoples in both Europe and Asia believed that the strength of any horned animal was centered in the two natural weapons with which it defended itself and attacked its enemies. So when that strength was concentrated in one great horn, as in the Indian rhino and the unicorn, it's easy to understand why people thought the horn was doubly powerful.

This may also explain why the rulers of ancient countries such as Assyria and Persia wore tall headdresses that came to a point like a horn. These headdresses were probably meant to demonstrate that the rulers, like unicorns, possessed extraordinary strength.

Standing priest-king figure with a pointed headdress. From the Hittite culture, North Syria, about 1600 B.C.

CHAPTER THREE

A Horse's Body, a Stag's Head, and an Elephant's Feet

MANY LATER GREEK and Roman writers read Ctesias's account of a unicorn. Some of them doubted the accuracy of his description. They went on to tell their readers about other kinds of unicorns that travelers had reported seeing in remote parts of the world. To us, these creatures will probably seem just as incredible as the animal Ctesias described, if not more so.

The Greek philosopher Aristotle (384–322 B.C.) dismissed Ctesias's account of a many-colored unicorn as mere foolishness. But he did not question the unicorn itself.

Ancient Egyptian wall relief showing farm scenes. At the left and middle of the top panel, note the oryx and the ibex, both of which are pictured with single horns. From the first half of the Sixth Dynasty, 2420–2300 B.C.

"There are some animals that have one horn only," Aristotle wrote. "For example, the oryx, whose hoof is cloven like a goat's, and the Indian ass, whose hoof is solid, like a horse's. Both of these creatures have their horn in the middle of their heads."

The oryx is a large African antelope with a pair of

long, straight horns. Why, then, did Aristotle think it had only one? He must not have seen the actual animal, but he may have seen representations of it in Egyptian wall paintings or reliefs. Most Egyptian paintings showed people and animals in profile, and when the oryx is depicted in profile it does seem to have a single horn.

Reports of unicorns came from other places besides India and Africa. In his book *The Conquest of Gaul*, the Roman general and statesman Julius Caesar (100–44 B.C.) told of unicorns that lived in the Hercynian Forest of Germany. This was a vast, thickly wooded area extending from the source of the Danube River in southwestern Germany all the way to what is now Czechoslovakia. It included what is today called the Black Forest.

According to Caesar, the Hercynian Forest was so big that "no western German claims to have reached its eastern extremity, even after traveling for two months, or to have heard where it ends." The forest contained many animals not seen elsewhere, Caesar said. For example, "There is an ox shaped like a stag, with a single horn in the middle of its forehead between the ears. This horn sticks up taller and straighter than those of the animals we know, and at the top it branches out widely like a man's hand or a tree."

From Caesar's description, this "ox shaped like a stag"

Julius Caesar's unicorn.

sounds very much like a reindeer. But why did Caesar think it had only one antler instead of two? We have no way of knowing.

The Roman naturalist Pliny the Elder (A.D. 23–79) may have read Julius Caesar's book, for he, too, wrote of a unicorn with a staglike head. But Pliny's unicorn, like Ctesias's, lived in India. "The Indians hunt many wild beasts," said Pliny, "the fiercest of which is the *monoceros* [meaning "one-horned" in Greek]. The monoceros has a body like a horse, a head like a stag, feet like an elephant, and a tail like a boar. It makes a deep bellow, and one black horn about three feet long projects from the middle of its forehead. This animal cannot be taken alive."

Obviously the travelers' tales of unicorns had gotten more extravagant. The unicorn Ctesias heard about had a foot-and-a-half-long horn, while the animal Pliny described had a horn twice that length. And the descriptions were to become even more exaggerated.

A later Roman writer on animals, Aelian (A.D. 170–235), offered his readers an account of not one but *two* different kinds of Indian unicorns. Some of the details seemed to come from Ctesias's writings, and others from Pliny's, but many were original with Aelian.

The first unicorn sounded similar to the one Ctesias

Pliny's unicorn.

had described. It was a one-horned ass with a white body, a dark-red head, and a horn that was part black, part white, and part crimson.

Aelian's second unicorn was a very different sort of creature. "In certain regions of India they say that there are impassable mountains filled with wild life," Aelian wrote. "In these regions there is said to exist a one-horned beast. It is the size of a full-grown horse, with reddish hair, and is very swift of foot. The creature has a mane like a lion, feet like an elephant's, and the tail of a goat. Between its eyebrows a horn grows out, black in color. This horn is said to be exceedingly sharp."

Aelian went on to describe the unicorn's mating habits. "It likes lonely grazing grounds where it roams in solitude, but at the mating season when it associates with the female, it becomes gentle and the two even graze side by side. They say that the foals when quite young are taken to the King and exhibit their strength against one another in public shows. But nobody remembers a full-grown animal having been captured."

Aelian may have based part of this description — especially of the horn — on one-horned Indian rhinos that he had seen. In the third century A.D., when Aelian lived, young specimens of various wild animals, including rhinos, were brought to Rome from the far corners of the Empire and

Aelian's second unicorn.

exhibited in the Circus Maximus. Some of the animals were trained to fight one another in Roman arenas, as Aelian described the young unicorns fighting at the palace of the Indian king.

Did Aelian and the other Greek and Roman writers have any doubts that unicorns really lived in India and other places? Apparently not. Although none of them had ever seen such an animal himself, they obviously believed the reports they'd heard from travelers, traders, and soldiers.

To us, the writers' descriptions of unicorns may seem farfetched. But to Aelian and other naturalists of his time, the unicorn was as credible as the camel, the giraffe, and the elephant. For they had seen few, if any, examples of these animals, either.

While Europeans were writing about the unicorns of India in greater and greater detail, the people of India, China, and other Far Eastern countries believed in unicorns that bore little resemblance to these creatures. In only one respect were the Oriental unicorns similar: They, too, were said to be endowed with amazing powers.

CHAPTER FOUR

The Ki-lin of China

BEFORE THERE WAS WRITING in China, people there told stories about unicorns and the remarkable gifts they had given to humanity.

According to one of these stories, an emperor named Fu Hsi ruled China almost 5,000 years ago. He was a wise and kind ruler who taught his people how to hunt, fish, and keep domestic animals. He even showed his subjects how to cook their food.

One day Emperor Fu Hsi was walking along the banks of the Yellow River when out of its waters rose a miraculous creature. It had the body of a deer, the tail of an ox, the head of a wolf, and the hooves of a horse. Out of its forehead grew a single horn, several feet long. And tied to its back was a large, rolled package.

The unicorn approached the emperor and knelt on the ground beside him. Turning its head, it indicated the package with its horn.

The emperor was amazed by the creature, and more than a little afraid, but he untied the package and opened it. Inside was a large roll of paper. The emperor spread it out on the ground and studied it. He saw that it was a map of his empire, with rivers and settlements identified by strange markings. What were they? The emperor looked at the markings more closely and realized that they must represent the names of the places on the map.

Puzzled, the emperor turned back toward the unicorn as if hoping it might somehow be able to explain the markings to him. But there was no trace of the mysterious creature; it had vanished as swiftly and silently as it had appeared.

The emperor carefully rolled up the map and returned with it to his palace. And that is how, according to the story, China acquired its written language.

While the ancient Greeks and Romans believed the uni-

A unicorn appears to Emperor Fu Hsi.

corn was a real animal, to the Chinese it was always a mythical beast like the one that appeared to Emperor Fu Hsi. The Chinese called the unicorn a *ki-lin* (pronounced chee-lin). This was a combination of their word for the male unicorn, *ki,* and the one for the female, *lin.* The male was described as having a horn while the female did not.

According to old Chinese writings, the *ki-lin* was one of the four superior creatures—three of them mythical, one of them real. The most important of the shelled animals was the very real tortoise. The phoenix, a mythical bird that was said to have lived for 500 years, burned itself to death, and risen again from its own ashes, was the leader of all feathered creatures. Among the scaly animals, first place was held by the dragon, in China a symbol of strength and goodness, not a fire-breathing monster. Last but far from least came the *ki-lin,* the unicorn, which was said to be the most worthy of all hairy animals.

As an indication of its importance, the *ki-lin*'s hair and skin included patches of all five of the sacred Chinese colors: red, yellow, blue, white, and black. It had a musical call that rang out like a monastery bell.

In Chinese tales, the *ki-lin* was said to be a solitary animal that lived in deep forests and high in the mountains. It never appeared to humans unless it came on a

Confucius's mother drapes a red ribbon over the ki-lin's *horn.*

special mission, like the one that brought the gift of writing to Emperor Fu Hsi.

Whenever a *ki-lin* showed itself to an emperor, it was thought the ruler would enjoy a long and peaceful reign. The Chinese also believed that *ki-lin*s appeared now and then to foretell the birth of great men like the philosopher Confucius.

There are several different versions of what happened when Confucius's pregnant mother saw the *ki-lin*. In one of them, she was walking in a wooded glade with two maids when a *ki-lin* suddenly materialized in front of her. Impressed by its strength and dignity, she took a red ribbon from her hair and draped it over the animal's horn.

The *ki-lin* seemed to be pleased with her gift. It walked around her slowly three times and then disappeared. Soon after, in about 550 B.C., the woman and her husband welcomed the birth of a son, whom they named Confucius.

In another version of the story, the *ki-lin* also appeared before Confucius's mother in a forest glade, but this time it held in its mouth a tablet made of jade. On the tablet was engraved a poem in praise of the man her son was to become. She took the tablet from the *ki-lin* and the animal immediately vanished. A few months later, she gave birth to Confucius, who, when he grew up, accomplished everything the poem had foretold.

Chinese enamel and copper container in the form of a ki-lin. *From the reign of Emperor Ch'ien Lung (1736–1795).*

Hearing tales such as these, many mothers-to-be in old China pasted pictures of the *ki-lin* on the walls of their rooms in hopes that they, too, would give birth to great men. And the Chinese gods who, it was believed, oversaw the distribution of babies were often portrayed riding on the back of a *ki-lin*.

The Buddhist religion spread to China from India in the first century A.D., and after that stories about the

ki-lin endowed the animal with many Buddhist virtues. Buddhists disapproved of the unnecessary taking of life. So it was said that the *ki-lin* refused to eat any living thing, animal or vegetable.

To preserve life, the Chinese unicorn would not step on an ant or even a blade of green grass. A soft, fleshy tip grew over the end of its horn so that the *ki-lin* could never use it to harm a living creature.

A Buddhist scholar writing in the second century A.D. summed up the virtues of the Chinese unicorn in these words: "The *ki-lin* often attains the age of a thousand years, and is the noblest form of animal creation, the emblem of perfect good."

The *ki-lin* was also known in ancient Japan, where it was called the *kirin*. The Japanese told many of the same stories about it that the Chinese did, but the *kirin* never attained the same popularity in Japan that the *ki-lin* enjoyed in China.

Meanwhile, in India, people told of a unicorn very different from either the *ki-lin* or the *kirin*. In fact, this Indian unicorn was unlike any other in the world.

CHAPTER FIVE

The Unicorn Man of India

THE UNICORN OF INDIA resembled neither a wild ass nor a rhinoceros. This unicorn wasn't even an animal; it was a handsome young man named Risharinga.

Risharinga first appeared in the pages of an Indian epic, *The Mahabharata,* that was written about 200 B.C. *Mahabharata* means "great story" in the Sanskrit language, and the book was a combination of myths and history. Many of the stories in it, including the one about the unicorn man, had been told and retold in India for hundreds of years before they were finally written down.

According to *The Mahabharata*, Risharinga's father was a Hindu holy man, Kasyapa. Tired of the world, Kasyapa decided to go off by himself and lead a life of poverty and meditation.

"Let him wander alone like a rhinoceros horn," said Kasyapa's friends. Their words were meant to be an encouragement to him. Since horns usually came in pairs, Kasyapa would be even more self-sufficient—and more religious—if he were like the single horn of the Indian rhinoceros, which, they believed, had the strength of two.

After journeying through a deep forest, Kasyapa came to the banks of the holy River Kausiki. There he built a hut for himself, and for many years he lived alone in it. When he was hungry, he went into the forest to gather wild fruits and nuts. Otherwise, he spent his days and nights in meditation.

One evening, just before sunset, a beautiful doe antelope appeared on the bank of the river near Kasyapa's hut. She seemed to be surrounded by a golden glow, and Kasyapa was captivated by her beauty. He approached her slowly, fearing she might turn and run away, but her eyes never left his.

The doe stayed with Kasyapa, and some months later she gave birth to a handsome baby son. He was formed like a human in all respects but one: From the middle of

Kasyapa, the doe antelope, and their newborn son.

his forehead grew a single horn curved like those of the male antelope.

Shortly after the baby was born, the doe became ill. She developed a high fever and within a few days she died despite all of Kasyapa's attempts to save her. The grief-stricken man was left to raise their son by himself. He named the boy Risharinga, meaning "antelope horn," and the child grew up never knowing any other human except his father.

When Risharinga was a young man, the land was ruled by an arrogant king named Lomapada. King Lomapada refused to listen to the advice of his priests and wise men and thought only of himself and his own pleasures. He amassed great wealth while his people went hungry.

As a result of the king's selfish actions, the gods became angry and caused all rains to stop. A terrible drought struck the land. The crops turned brown and died, and when King Lomapada sent out his stewards to obtain provisions for the palace, they came back empty-handed.

In despair, the king turned to his priests and wise men and asked them what he should do. One said: "Send for Risharinga, the hermit's son, the one with a horn growing out of his forehead. He is a forest child, ignorant of the ways of the world, and devoted to uprightness. If he comes to your kingdom, the gods will relent and cause heavy rains to fall once more."

"How will I persuade Risharinga to come?" asked the king.

"Send your daughter, Shanta, up the River Kausiki in a boat laden with flowers and fruit," said the wise man. "Risharinga has never seen a woman, and he will be charmed by her."

"But Shanta is my only child!" protested the king. "How can I send her on such a mission?"

"Only a beautiful maiden like Shanta will be successful," said the wise man, and at last the king was convinced. A magnificent boat was stocked with every luxury, and Shanta set sail up the river in search of Risharinga. The girl was fearful, but she knew the lives of her people and her country were at stake.

As the boat neared the spot where Risharinga lived, the princess saw a young man picking berries from a patch of bushes on the riverbank. He was a tall, handsome youth dressed in the simple clothes of a hermit. But the curving horn that grew from his forehead marked him as Risharinga. The princess ordered the sailors to moor the boat, and she stepped gracefully ashore.

When Risharinga looked up and saw Shanta, he was struck by her beauty as his father had been struck by the beauty of the doe. He offered her berries from his basket, and the princess took a handful. She, in turn, offered him fruit from the boat, and a cool, delicious drink.

After they had finished eating, the princess got a ball from the boat and tossed it to Risharinga. For a moment he was confused; he had never played with a ball before. Then he tossed it back to Shanta.

She plucked flowers from a vine and twined them around Risharinga's horn. By now she had become used to the horn, and even found it attractive. She stood on tiptoe to give Risharinga a kiss. Then she stepped aboard her boat and sailed back the way she had come.

Risharinga went home able to think of nothing but the beautiful princess. When his father returned to the hut from gathering wild fruit in the forest, he told him all about Shanta.

Kasyapa was furious, and called her a temptress. He forbade Risharinga to see her again and made the youth promise to expel all thoughts of her from his mind. But Risharinga could not. He lay awake that night, seeing again Shanta's face and the silken garments she wore, and hearing her laugh as she tossed the ball to him.

When his father went off into the forest the next day to gather more fruit, Risharinga waited until he was out of sight and then hurried along the riverbank in search of Shanta. A few miles downriver, he found her boat at anchor. She was overjoyed to see him and invited him aboard the boat. They sailed away together before Risharinga's

Princess Shanta and Risharinga.

father could return and prevent his son from going.

As they neared her kingdom, Risharinga told the princess how much he loved her. She, in turn, confessed why she had sought him out in the first place. He was upset and angry until she took his hands and assured him that she loved him as much as he loved her.

Then Shanta pointed out the terrible sights to be seen on both sides of the river—the dried-up farmyards, the abandoned houses, the animals lying dead in the fields. Gazing at all the devastation, Risharinga wept tears of sorrow and compassion. At that very moment, a hard, soaking rain began to fall, just as the wise man had predicted.

When Risharinga and Shanta arrived at the palace, her father, the king, was startled at first. He had never seen anything like the single horn that grew out of the young man's forehead. But then the king remembered the good deed Risharinga had performed. He announced to everyone present that he would give his daughter in marriage to the unicorn man in gratitude for his having saved the country.

Hearing the king's words, Risharinga and the princess clasped hands delightedly.

The king also announced that when Risharinga's father came in search of his son, he should be told that all the

cows and crops in the rain-refreshed fields were Risharinga's. And the unicorn man could dispense this wealth
in any charitable way he wished.

This was done, and Kasyapa's anger had cooled by the
time he reached the palace. There he joined in the wedding
celebrations for Risharinga and the princess, and they all
lived happily from that time onward.

The gentle unicorn man provided a fine example of
Hindu religious ideals in action. We may wonder how
Risharinga's mother could be a doe antelope, but Hindu
readers and listeners would have understood that she was
a divine maiden who had been put under a curse by evil
spirits. Such transformations happen frequently in Hindu
literature, just as they do in European fairy tales. Hindus
would also have recognized that Risharinga's horn sym-
bolized the divine qualities of sensitivity and compassion
that he had inherited from his mother.

While Indian Hindus were reading and enjoying the
story of Risharinga, a very different kind of unicorn
entered the pages of the Judeo-Christian Bible for the
first time. How and why did it get there? No one knows
for certain, but it may have been by mistake.

CHAPTER SIX

A Maiden Tames the Unicorn

"HIS GLORY IS LIKE the firstling of his bullock, and his horns are like the horns of unicorns: with them he shall push the people together to the ends of the earth." Deut. 33:17.

That is the way the King James Bible describes Joseph, one of the early leaders of the Jews. The reference to his having horns was not meant to be taken literally; it was just a poetic way of suggesting Joseph's strength.

Nor were the horns necessarily compared with the single, powerful horn of the unicorn in the original Hebrew version of the Old Testament. A group of seventy-two scholars living in Alexandria, Egypt, in about the second century B.C. introduced that idea when they made a new translation of the Old Testament into Greek. This translation is known as the *Septuagint,* meaning "seventy," because it was supposed to have been completed in just seventy days.

In the original version, the Hebrew writers referred seven times to a powerful animal called the *re'em.* One of these references appeared in the description of Joseph that was quoted earlier. Not knowing what animal the Hebrews had in mind, the authors of the *Septuagint* translated *re'em* as *monoceros,* the Greek word for "unicorn."

There's no reason to believe, however, that the Hebrews thought of the *re'em* as one-horned. Some later scholars argued that it was probably the African antelope, the oryx. They pointed out that the Arabic word for oryx was the similar *rim.*

Others thought the Hebrews meant the giant aurochs, a species of wild ox that became extinct in the sixteenth century. From fossil remains that have been found, scientists estimate that this great beast was at least twelve feet long and seven feet tall, and boasted a magnificent pair of horns. If the Hebrews had wanted a symbol of power and strength, they couldn't have found a better one than the aurochs.

Why then did the translators of the *Septuagint* choose the unicorn instead? There can be no definite answer to that question. Perhaps they had read accounts of the wondrous animal by Ctesias and other writers, and decided that the unicorn was the most likely candidate.

Whatever the reason, their choice was to have a lasting impact on later Christian scholars, and on the religious beliefs of the Middle Ages. For the *Septuagint,* like the original books of the Old Testament, was thought to be divinely inspired. Thus it seemed that God himself had confirmed the existence of the unicorn.

The unicorn appeared in another book that people read and enjoyed in the Near East and Europe for more than a thousand years. Written originally in Greek, it was a collection of legends and factual information about forty real and imaginary animals.

This book was called the *Physiologus* because each chapter describing a particular animal began "The physiologus [the scientist] says. . . ." The book proved to be so popular that it was translated into a dozen languages and the text was expanded to include more than sixty additional animals. By the twelfth century, the enlarged versions of the *Physiologus* were known in western Europe as bestiaries. A bestiary was a book of beasts.

Above: A manticore. Below: An amphisbena.

Real animals like the lion, the camel, and the weasel marched through the pages of the bestiaries alongside such fanciful creatures as the manticore. This animal was described as having the face of a man with blood-red eyes, the body of a lion, and a tail like a scorpion's stinger. The manticore was able to leap so high that even the tallest barrier could not contain it. And it had an enormous appetite for human flesh.

Another remarkable creature in the bestiaries was the amphisbena. It was a snake with two heads, one in the proper place and the other in its tail. When one head held on to the other with its teeth, the amphisbena could roll along a path like a hoop. It was also said that one of the amphisbena's heads would wake up the other when it was that head's turn to watch over the creature's newly hatched eggs.

Next to strange beasts like the manticore and the amphisbena, the unicorn seems almost as believable as the horse or the dog. Here is how it was described in a ninth-century bestiary that was published in Switzerland: "The unicorn is a small animal, like a young goat, but surprisingly fierce for his size. He has one very sharp horn on his head, and no hunter is able to take him by force.

"Yet there is a trick by which he can be captured. Hunters lead a maiden to the place where the unicorn is

THE CLEVELAND MUSEUM OF ART, JOHN L. SEVERANCE FUND, 78.39.

Ivory panel from a casket showing hunting scenes. In the middle left section, a unicorn has laid its head in the lap of a maiden. Above it, a hunter kneels on a tree branch, ready to plunge his spear into the unicorn's flank. From France or Germany, first half of the fourteenth century.

most often found and leave her there alone. As soon as he sees this maiden, the unicorn runs up and lays his head tenderly in her lap. The hunters then approach and seize him and lead him to the palace of the king."

Here, for the first time, a maiden enters the unicorn legend in the West. From now on, whether in medieval works of art or in modern stories about unicorns, she will almost always play a leading role.

Where did this maiden come from? No one can be

entirely sure, but scholars know that the authors of the *Physiologus* drew on many Far Eastern legends when they were compiling their book. Perhaps some of them had read and remembered the Indian story of Risharinga. Its account of how the princess gets the unicorn man to return with her to the palace of her father, the king, is certainly similar to the way the maiden attracts the unicorn in the *Physiologus.*

The authors of the *Physiologus* and the bestiaries did not stop with a simple description of each animal included. Like Aesop, they went on to point out lessons that could be learned from the creature's habits and characteristics. In the case of the unicorn, these lessons emerged from a startling comparison that the authors of the bestiaries made. To them, the small, fierce, one-horned animal was a symbol for Jesus Christ.

According to the authors, the unicorn's single horn represented the unity between Jesus and God the Father. The animal's defiance of the hunters reminded people of Jesus's refusal to bow down before his enemies. And the unicorn's small size exemplified the humility of Christ, who became a vulnerable human being for the sake of mankind.

The authors even found a way to relate the maiden to the story of Jesus. Just as the unicorn lost its fierceness and was tamed by means of the maiden, they wrote, so Jesus surrendered his divine nature and became a vulnerable human being by means of the Virgin Mary.

It doesn't seem to have occurred to the authors of the bestiaries that the maiden who aided the hunters in capturing the unicorn may not have been an admirable person. If she deliberately set out to deceive the unicorn, she certainly wasn't a likely symbol for the Virgin Mary, who would never have deceived her own son. But this obviously didn't bother the countless medieval writers who linked the unicorn and the maiden with Jesus and Mary.

One of the most unusual of these writers was the German nun Hildegarde of Bingen, who lived from 1098 to 1179. From an early age, Hildegarde experienced remarkable visions of the past, present, and future that her priest encouraged her to write down.

During her long life Hildegarde wrote many other works: biographies of the saints of the Roman Catholic Church, and two books on medical and natural history topics that combined fanciful material with accurate scientific observation. In them, Hildegarde had a number of things to say about unicorns.

Like the Greek writer Ctesias, whose books she may have read, Hildegarde thought parts of the unicorn could be used for medicinal purposes. (We should keep in mind that in Hildegarde's time Europeans not only believed in unicorns but also had a limited knowledge of medical science.) Shoes made of unicorn hide would assure healthy

feet and legs, Hildegarde wrote. A belt crafted of unicorn leather would keep away fevers and the plague. Unicorn liver, ground up and mixed with egg yolk, was a sure cure for leprosy.

Hildegarde, like other medieval writers, believed that the unicorn was a symbol of Jesus. But in a description of a mythical unicorn hunt, she offered a different version of how the animal was captured. Instead of a single maiden luring the unicorn to its doom, many young women were involved—and apparently they weren't at all aware of what they were doing.

"On the day of the hunt, men, women, and young girls pursue the unicorn," wrote Hildegarde. "Then the girls separate from the others and go off to gather flowers in a meadow. The unicorn, upon seeing the girls, stops at once, crouches on his hind legs in the tall grass, and watches them for a long time. He falls in love with the girls, for he sees that they are gentle and kind. But while he is gazing at them, the hunters steal up behind and slay the unicorn and cut off his horn."

While some Europeans speculated about how unicorns could be captured, others reported new sightings of the animal in various parts of the world.

Marco Polo, a young trader from the Italian city of Venice, made several journeys to faraway China in the

Hildegarde of Bingen's version of a unicorn hunt.

late thirteenth century. At that time, few Europeans knew anything about China, and an even smaller number had ever actually traveled there.

Polo became a favorite of the Chinese ruler Kublai Khan, who sent him on several missions within the country and to the states of Southeast Asia. Back in Italy, Polo wrote an account of his experiences. It described the places he had visited or heard about, the customs of the inhabitants, and the unusual birds and animals that lived in each one.

One of these places was Sumatra, a large island in Southeast Asia. On it, Polo reported, a strange kind of unicorn could be found. "There are wild elephants on that island," he wrote, "and numerous unicorns which are very nearly as big. They have hair like that of the buffalo, feet like those of the elephant, and a horn in the middle of the forehead which is black and very thick.

"The head resembles that of the wild boar," Polo continued, "and they carry it always bent to the ground. They delight in wallowing in mire and mud. 'Tis an ugly beast to look upon," he added, "and not in the least like the unicorn our stories tell us of, the fierce creature that is caught in the lap of a maiden. In fact, it is altogether different from our fancies."

Polo may have been disappointed with this muddy unicorn. But without knowing it, he gave his readers

Engraving of various animals found in India, including the one-horned rhinoceros. From the book Peregrinations in India, *published in Germany in 1601.*

their first detailed description of the one-horned rhinoceros.

Most representations of the unicorn in Polo's time and later were drawn and painted along more traditional lines. Some portrayed an animal with a goat's beard on a horse's head. Other unicorns had a horselike head atop a goat's small body. Almost all the unicorns had the cloven hooves of a goat.

Because of their association with Jesus, unicorns that

looked like this frequently appeared in European church decorations. From England to France to Germany, they could be found carved in the backs of choir stalls and pictured on stained-glass windows.

Nonreligious artists included images of the unicorn in their works also. Many of the aquamaniles (vessels containing water) that medieval nobles and clergy used in washing their hands were cast in the form of unicorns. Artists drew pictures of unicorns in the margins of hand-painted books. Craftsmen carved them in wood and ivory on the sides of jewel boxes and chests.

Unicorns were also featured in the magnificent tapestries that kings and nobles hung on the walls of their castles and mansions. A famous series of French tapestries, *The Unicorn and the Maiden*, depicted the five senses. In the one representing sight, the gentle, goatlike unicorn was looking at itself in a mirror held by the maiden. In the tapestry portraying touch, the maiden had her hand around the unicorn's horn.

But the most famous—and many would say the best-loved—of all the tapestries featuring unicorns were the seven known collectively as *The Hunt of the Unicorn*, or simply the Unicorn Tapestries. They brought together all the wondrous qualities that medieval people associated with the unicorn. They also gave the world an image of the unicorn that would endure for centuries to come.

Bronze aquamanile in the form of a unicorn. German, about 1400.

CHAPTER SEVEN

The Unicorn in the Tapestries

ON THE SURFACE, the story the Unicorn Tapestries tell seems simple and straightforward. In seven separate panels, each of which was originally about fourteen feet high and twelve feet wide, a band of hunters tracks and kills a handsome white unicorn and brings its dead body back to a castle. Then, in the final tapestry, the unicorn miraculously returns to life.

Beneath the surface of the story, though, lie many hidden meanings that would have been obvious to medieval people, but are not so obvious to us. And beyond

The
HUNT
of the
UNICORN

SIX TAPESTRIES
AND TWO FRAGMENTS
OF A SEVENTH.
FRANCO-FLEMISH,
FROM ABOUT THE YEAR 1500.

The Metropolitan Museum of Art,
The Cloisters Collection,
Gift of John D. Rockefeller, Jr., 1937-1938.

I. "The Start of the Hunt."

II. *"The Unicorn Dips His Horn into the Stream to Rid It of Poison."*

III. "The Unicorn Leaps the Stream."

IV. "The Unicorn Defends Himself."

V. *"The Unicorn Is Tamed by the Maiden."* (*Two fragments, showing a hunter at the left and a friend of the maiden signaling to him at the right. Note the hand of the maiden stroking the unicorn's mane.*)

VI. "The Unicorn Is Killed and Brought to the Castle."

VII. "The Unicorn in Captivity."

that, there are other mysteries connected with the tapestries themselves. For example, no one knows exactly where they were made, or for whom. But an item of clothing worn by the men in the tapestries does give us a good idea of when they were made.

At the end of the fifteenth century, Frenchmen gave up the pointed shoes that had been fashionable for several decades in favor of more comfortable shoes and boots with blunt, square toes. Since many of the huntsmen in the tapestries are wearing square-toed boots, we can assume that the Unicorn Tapestries were woven sometime between 1485 and the early 1500s, when men's shoe styles changed again.

No written records exist concerning the weaving of the tapestries. But the quality of the workmanship leads experts to think they were made in Brussels, Belgium. During the Middle Ages, the tapestry workshops of Brussels were famous throughout Europe.

There's no record of who ordered the tapestries, either. The first time they were mentioned was in an inventory of the Duke of La Rochefoucauld's possessions, taken after he died in Paris in 1680. Since the letters *F* and *R*, tied together with a bowknot, appear on the third tapestry, some experts believe the *R* stands for Rochefoucauld. If they are correct, the tapestries were probably woven for a member of the Rochefoucauld family who lived in the 1490s, and whose first name was François.

Confusing the issue, though, are the letters *A* and *E,* also linked by a knot, that can be seen on all seven of the tapestries. There is no apparent connection between these letters and any member of the Rochefoucauld family living in the 1400s. However, medieval people delighted in mysterious combinations of letters, secret ciphers, and codes understood only by them and a few close friends. Perhaps the linked *A* and *E* were a secret code devised by someone in the La Rochefoucauld family.

The knot that ties the letters together suggests another possible answer. In the Middle Ages, this type of knot was known as a "link of love," and often was used to indicate a married couple. This leads some experts to think that the letters *A* and *E* stood for a Latin expression such as *Amor in eternum* ("Love eternal") or the French expression *Amour et esperance* ("Love and hope"). These experts go on to speculate that the tapestries were a wedding gift from a member of the La Rochefoucauld family to his bride.

The designer of the tapestries remains a mystery today also. Whoever it was must have read or heard all of the ancient lore concerning the unicorn. He was also familiar with medieval beliefs about other beasts and birds, and

Detail from "The Start of the Hunt," the first of the tapestries in the Hunt of the Unicorn *series. Note the linked letters* A *and* E *in the bottom right-hand corner. The* E *is reversed for the sake of the design.*

the symbolic meanings assigned to certain flowers and trees. But he obviously possessed an active imagination of his own, for he had the original idea of combining the chief elements in the unicorn legend with the events of a medieval stag hunt.

In the first tapestry, three elegantly dressed huntsmen enter a forest carpeted with wildflowers. The one in the middle, who has a hunting horn strapped over his shoulder, is no doubt the lord of the manor. The other two are probably his guests. They carry spears, indicating that the beast they seek is dangerous.

The keepers of the dogs walk ahead of the huntsmen, their animals leashed. As in medieval stag hunts, two types of dogs participate: slender greyhounds that chase mainly by sight, and blunt-nosed running hounds that hunt by scent. A scout hiding in a grove of trees in the upper right corner of the tapestry raises a hand. This lets the hunters know that their quarry, the unicorn, has been sighted.

The unicorn appears for the first time in the second tapestry. He crouches before a fountain from which water flows into a narrow stream. Bending his horselike head, he dips his spiraled horn into the stream while a gathering of animals—two lions, a tiger, a hyena, and a stag— wait patiently. Behind the animals, a large group of hunters, including those from the first tapestry, pauses to watch the scene. According to the rules of the stag hunt, they must wait until their quarry starts to run before they give chase.

Why is the unicorn dipping his horn in the stream? And what are the other animals waiting for? The answers to these questions can be found in a Greek bestiary written sometime between the twelfth and fourteenth centuries. It includes the following tale, which the designer of the Unicorn Tapestries must have been familiar with since the scene he planned dramatizes it almost line by line.

"There is a stream where the animals gather to drink," said the bestiary. "But before they have assembled, the serpent comes and casts its poison into the water. The animals mark well the poison and do not dare to drink and they wait for the unicorn. He comes and immediately goes into the stream and, dipping his horn in the water, renders the poison harmless. Then he drinks, and all of the other animals drink as well."

The meaning of this tale would be clear to all medieval people who had read or listened to the bestiaries. The serpent is the Devil, who brought the poison of sin into the world when he tempted Eve with the apple in the Garden of Eden. And the unicorn is Jesus Christ, whose words and actions redeemed the world from sin according to Christian belief.

A detail in the second tapestry reinforces the notion that the set of seven may have been woven as a wedding gift. This is the presence of a lion and a lioness among the animals at the stream. In the bestiaries, it was often said that the lion took only one mate, to whom he was forever faithful. If a bridegroom ordered the tapestries, the inclusion of a lion and a lioness was probably meant to indicate that he, like the lion, would always be faithful to his bride.

In the third tapestry, the chase is on. Like a stag, the unicorn enters a small river in an attempt to throw the dogs off his track. But he is not successful. Three of the running hounds pursue him in the water and a pair of greyhounds is close on his heels also. Several of the hunters aim their spears at the unicorn, but he eludes them for the moment by leaping onto the riverbank.

The unicorn looks the same in this tapestry as he does in all the others, but the hunters do not. A few of them can be followed from panel to panel, but others seem to come and go. No one knows why the designer decided to change the cast of characters so often. Perhaps he enjoyed creating a wide variety of personalities, dressed in an equally wide variety of clothing, and believed his medieval viewers would enjoy looking at them also.

Hunters and dogs surround the unicorn in the fourth tapestry and close in for the kill. Even though there is little chance of escape, the unicorn—like those described by ancient writers—fights back fiercely. He slashes a greyhound with his horn while at the same time kicking a hunter with both of his hind legs. It would be hard to find anywhere in art a more heroic unicorn than the one portrayed in this tapestry.

Only two fragments remain of the fifth panel in the series. No one knows what happened to the rest of it over the centuries. However, these fragments give us a good idea of what the complete tapestry pictured. Obviously the unicorn did manage to escape from the hunters, and now—as in the bestiaries—he has been tamed by a maiden.

All we see of the maiden is her brown-sleeved arm and hand. The hand is patting the unicorn's neck while a greyhound and a running hound paw at the animal's back. The unicorn seems totally unaware of the danger he is in. He gazes lovingly at the missing maiden and even seems to be smiling. In the background, another young woman signals to a hunter that the unicorn can now be seized.

This scene takes place in a garden surrounded by a fence covered with red and white roses. To people of the

Middle Ages, both the enclosed garden and the roses had symbolic meanings, and both were associated with the Virgin Mary.

The white roses stood for Mary's purity and virginity, the red roses for her charity. The garden itself was symbolic of Mary also. As a medieval writer, Bernard of Clairvaux, said: "Mary is a garden enclosed because she is a valley of charity that is sealed, into which nothing evil can break."

Knowing these meanings, the designer of the tapestries had a special reason for putting the unicorn and the maiden within a rose-covered enclosure. He wanted to remind medieval viewers of the close connection between the two of them and Jesus and Mary.

The sixth tapestry combines two separate scenes and brings the story of the unicorn hunt to its tragic climax. In the upper left corner, the hunters stab the unicorn to death. Unlike some other scenes in medieval art, this one does not happen while the unicorn's head is still in the maiden's lap. Instead, as in a stag hunt, the killing occurs somewhere else and the maiden is nowhere to be seen.

The rest of the sixth tapestry shows the hunters bringing the body of the unicorn back to a castle. Waiting for them outside the gate are the lord and lady of the castle, accompanied by their friends and servants. The lady is dressed in brown, as was the maiden who tamed the unicorn. Perhaps they were one and the same; we will never know unless the rest of the fifth tapestry is found someday. And perhaps the lady and the lord are portraits of the engaged couple for whom the tapestries may have been woven. Again, we can't be sure.

One of the returning hunters grasps the dead unicorn's horn and points in the direction of the lord. By this gesture, he seems to be saying that the lord will receive the horn as the prize of the hunt.

The unicorn's head is garlanded with oak branches. Crowns of oak leaves were often awarded to victorious generals in ancient and medieval times. The oak garland on the unicorn's head may have been designed to indicate how bravely he fought against the hunters.

Oddly, the garland has thorns, which the oak does not possess in nature. They were put there to remind people of the crown of thorns that Jesus wore, and to emphasize yet again the link between Christ and the unicorn.

The seventh and last tapestry is unlike the others in many ways, although it has always been listed in inventories with them. This tapestry bears no relation to a medieval stag hunt, nor is it realistic in style like the six that preceded it. The seventh tapestry shows the unicorn alive again. He seems to be quite happy although he is chained to a fanciful fruit tree in another enclosed garden.

Some say the peaceful-looking animal symbolizes the resurrected Christ. They point out that the unicorn, like Jesus, was pursued by his enemies, captured, and killed. Now he has been brought to life again, and rests contentedly in a heavenly garden of a thousand flowers.

The tree in the enclosed garden resembles no known variety, but its fruits are clearly those of the pomegranate. In this tapestry, the unicorn appears to be bleeding still from the wounds dealt him by the hunters. But the stains are really blood-red pomegranate seeds and juice dripping down onto his white coat. This reinforces the idea that the unicorn represents Jesus. For to medieval minds the pomegranate was a symbol of Christ, and also of immortality.

Since the unicorn is fenced and collared, other experts think he stands not only for Jesus, but also for the bridegroom who may have ordered the tapestries. According to this interpretation, the groom was chained by love to his bride just as the unicorn is chained to the tree. The couple's marriage was like a beautiful enclosed garden. And the pomegranate fruits with their many seeds expressed the pair's hope that they would be blessed with many children.

Whatever the unicorn stood for, its portrayal in the

Unicorn Tapestries demonstrated what an important role it played in the imaginations of medieval men and women. And not just their imaginations. For most people of the time still believed that unicorns lived in remote, unexplored corners of the world.

Strengthening this belief were the rare and mysterious horns that began to appear in European markets as early as the thirteenth century. The merchants who offered them for sale claimed they were genuine unicorn horns.

Made of ivory, the horns were straight whereas those of most animals were curved. Some of the hollow horns were more than seven feet long and weighed as much as twenty pounds. Unlike other horns, they had spirals running down their entire length, just like the horn of the unicorn in the tapestries.

But were the long, straight horns really those of unicorns? If not, what unknown creature did they come from?

CHAPTER EIGHT

The Unicorn of the Sea

IN THE YEAR 1126, a Danish ship returning from far northern waters was caught in a terrible storm off Iceland. It broke apart and sank, drowning everyone aboard.

The bodies of sailors and goods from the ship's hold washed up in a marsh along the shore. There they were found by people from a nearby village, who ever afterward called the place the Pool of Corpses.

Among the items the villagers salvaged were several long white horns, each with a sailor's name written on it. The villagers had never seen anything like the spiraled ivory horns and guessed that they must be very valuable. They were right. For these were examples of the horns that merchants in London, Paris, Florence, and other European cities were advertising as unicorn horns.

The above story, which appeared in an early history of Iceland, is the first real indication of an active trade in the horns. The merchants involved kept almost no written records, perhaps because they didn't want their customers to know where the horns came from. Besides, it wasn't a very large or regular trade. At its height in the fifteenth and sixteenth centuries, there were probably no more than fifty complete "unicorn horns" of this type in all of Europe and Great Britain. As a result, they commanded very high prices.

In the late fifteenth century, a complete horn was worth more than twice its weight in gold. Kings, nobles, and high church officials all sought to possess one of the precious objects. The Holy Roman Emperor Charles V, who ruled between 1519 and 1556, gave a German noble two horns as payment for a debt equal to a million dollars in today's money. When Queen Elizabeth I came to the throne of England in 1558, an inventory was taken of the royal treasury and its one unicorn horn was valued at 10,000 pounds. In Elizabeth's day, that amount would buy a large country

Cup made of "unicorn horn." Danish, 1660. Note the miniature unicorns on which the cup rests, and the Eskimo hunter sitting atop the handle.

estate with a castle on it.

It wasn't just their rarity that made the horns so valuable. Like the unicorn horns described by Ctesias and other ancient writers, they were thought to be one of the best protections against poison.

The danger that someone might poison them was taken very seriously by wealthy and powerful Europeans. Physicians of the time lacked the means to detect the presence of a poison in the body, and did not know exactly how various poisons affected the internal organs. Consequently, ruthless nobles like the Borgia family in Italy often arranged to have their enemies poisoned with arsenic and other substances. It was usually the swiftest and safest means of getting rid of anyone who stood in their way.

Because even small pieces of unicorn horn sold for high prices, unscrupulous merchants sometimes tried to substitute the bones of dogs, pigs, or fossil animals for the genuine article. To guard against this practice, potential buyers devised elaborate tests that were supposed to prove whether the horns were true or false.

In one test, a piece of horn was placed under a covered dish with three or more live, poisonous scorpions. Four hours later the cover was removed. If the scorpions were dead or nearly so, then the horn was assumed to be the real thing.

Another test performed in Italy involved two pigeons. First, both pigeons were given a fatal dose of arsenic in their food. Then scrapings were taken from the unicorn horn that was being tested. One of the pigeons was fed as many of the scrapings as it could swallow; the other pigeon received none. After displaying a few symptoms of sickness, the first pigeon revived and lived. The second pigeon died within two hours. According to the testers, this proved without a doubt that the horn in question was genuine. But so far as is known, there were no independent observers present to verify the results.

Once a horn had passed the test, whatever it was, it could be used by its new owner in any number of ways. Sometimes he had goblets, cups, or bowls carved from it. If a poisoned liquid touched the vessel, people believed it would "froth darkly and be cleansed," as one writer on medicine put it.

Often a horn was set in the middle of the dining table before a meal. Should any dishes on the table contain poisoned food, it was believed the horn would break out in a kind of sweat. When this happened, the dishes were instantly removed and others substituted for them.

As a further precaution, a servant might carry the horn around the table and touch each dish and pitcher with it before any of the guests ate or drank. An entire horn wasn't necessary for this. One king of France had a small piece of horn mounted on a chain of gilded silver. Each time the king's glass was refilled, a servant dipped the piece of horn into the wine to make sure it was safe.

Until the Revolution in 1789, the eating utensils of all

the kings of France were made of so-called unicorn horns. Craftsmen in other countries fitted slices of horn into the handles of table knives. They shaped the horn into "test-spoons" that were used in puddings and stews.

Most poor people of the time did not live in fear of being poisoned. However, they took small quantities of powdered horn as a medicine. Pharmacists claimed it would cure everything from a stomachache to rabies to smallpox.

In the meantime, European seafarers were venturing farther and farther into unexplored regions of the world. After Columbus's pioneering voyage to the New World in 1492, the Portuguese explorer Vasco da Gama became the first European to journey by sea to India. Between 1497 and 1499, da Gama sailed down the west coast of Africa, rounded the Cape of Good Hope, continued up the east coast of Africa, and sailed across the Indian Ocean to India.

Neither da Gama nor the sailors who accompanied him reported seeing any unicorns during the course of the voyage. Nor did Ferdinand Magellan, another Portuguese navigator, who between 1519 and 1521 led the first expedition to sail around South America and on across the Pacific. But a British sea captain, Martin Frobisher, announced an amazing discovery when he returned to London from an Arctic voyage in 1577. He claimed to have found a sea unicorn, and he had the evidence to prove it.

Frobisher had been searching for a northern sea route to Asia when he ran into a fierce summer storm in the waters off Baffin Island. His three battered ships sought shelter from the storm in an inlet now known as Frobisher Bay. There, floating in an icy pool along the shore, the captain and his men found the body of "a great dead fish."

Frobisher described the "fish" as being "round like a porpoise, and about twelve feet long." However, the most unusual thing about the creature was its single, spiraled horn. According to Frobisher, the horn grew out of the fish's snout and was "two yards long lacking two inches."

Since people in Frobisher's time believed that every land animal had its counterpart in the sea, the captain decided his discovery must be a sea unicorn. To make certain, his men removed the creature's horn and put it to one of the standard tests. They placed some poisonous spiders inside the hollow horn and sealed it shut. When they opened the horn several hours later, the spiders were dead—or so the sailors reported to Frobisher. Gleefully he wrote in his log, "Now the creature can truly be said to be the sea unicorn!"

Actually, Frobisher was far from being the first European to discover a sea creature with a single horn. The horns found in Iceland's Pool of Corpses 400 years earlier came from the same marine animal. The Danish seamen who traded the horns in European markets had even given the animal a name. They called it the *narhval,* or "corpse whale," because its white underside reminded them of a dead body. In English, the word was spelled "narwhal."

However, so far as we know, Frobisher was the first European to describe the creature in detail. On his return to England he proudly presented its impressive horn to Queen Elizabeth I. It was given a place of honor in her treasury of jewels and precious objects, alongside the other "unicorn horn" she had inherited when she came to the throne.

To some, there had never been more convincing proof than Frobisher's horn that the unicorn existed. But even before his discovery, other European thinkers had begun to raise serious new questions about the creature.

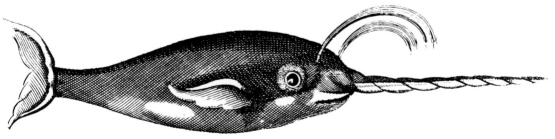

AMERICAN MUSEUM OF NATURAL HISTORY.

Engraving of a narwhal from an eighteenth-century book about sea creatures. The artist shows two jets of water coming out of the narwhal's blowholes.

CHAPTER NINE

Doubters and Believers

AS A RESULT OF the great voyages of discovery in the sixteenth century, a new interest in science began to spread throughout Europe. Many "truths" that people had held since ancient times were questioned, among them belief in the unicorn.

In 1566, an Italian scholar, Andrea Marini, reread all the different descriptions people over the centuries had given of the unicorn. After lining them up, he wondered if any of these people had ever actually seen the fabled creature.

Next, Marini compared the ivory of "unicorn horns" he had viewed in cathedrals with the ivory in walrus tusks. Afterward, he said he believed the horns also belonged to a marine animal. (This was eleven years before Frobisher discovered his sea unicorn.)

Going further, Marini doubted whether the horns were an effective defense against poisons. He didn't know where that notion had come from, but thought it probably could be traced back to the custom of kings in ancient times who drank from vessels made of horn.

"Even today," Marini wrote, "those princes who live in constant fear keep on their tables pieces of unicorn horn. They pretend—or perhaps they really believe without any evidence—that the horns will sweat when poison is brought near." He went on to say that this was impossible. Being solid and lifeless, the horns could not sweat. Only living things were capable of sweating.

Marini hoped his words would crush this superstition, and that "men of sense will in future leave the unicorn to charlatans and use more trustworthy protections against poison."

Not everyone was convinced, however. In the same year that Marini's book appeared, another Italian writer, Andrea Bacci, wrote a book defending the unicorn against Marini's charges. Bacci was a physician to the

Pope and several members of the powerful Medici family. Some suggested that he wrote his book at the urging of his patients, all of whom had large sums of money invested in unicorn horns.

In any event, Bacci argued that the fact that few if any people had ever actually seen a unicorn did not prove its nonexistence, but only its rarity. Since it was so rare, the unicorn and its horn would naturally be of great value. And it wasn't surprising that the horn possessed miraculous powers, including the ability to detect poisons.

So far as we know, Bacci never tested a horn by setting it beside a poison to see if it would sweat. He obviously didn't think that was important. "Whether the unicorn's horn sweats or does not sweat," he wrote, "the belief that it does will do no injury to truth, and will be for the good of the state." In other words, it would be good for all the wealthy nobles who owned unicorn horns.

Other scholars showed a greater interest in scientific evidence where the unicorn was concerned. One of them was Ambroise Paré, a French physician who has often been called the "father of modern surgery."

In 1580, Paré treated a nobleman for an infection caused by a fall from a horse. The nobleman, who had heard that powder from a unicorn horn was a sure cure for such infections, was surprised when Paré did not prescribe

THE ROYAL DANISH COLLECTIONS AT ROSENBORG PALACE, COPENHAGEN.

Another cup made of "unicorn horn." Danish, 1663. Note the Eskimo hunter standing atop the lid, a narwhal tusk in his left hand.

it. He asked Paré why he hadn't, and the physician's answer eventually became a book.

Like Marini, Paré questioned the very existence of the unicorn. "If it were not for the fact that it is mentioned in the Bible," Paré wrote, "I should not think that such a creature as the unicorn ever lived."

But the Bible said nothing about the medicinal powers of unicorn horns, and Paré put examples of these to various scientific tests. First he drew circles on a table with water in which a piece of horn had been soaked for hours. Then he placed several scorpions and poisonous spiders on the table. They simply ignored the lines Paré had drawn, crossing and recrossing them without being harmed in any way.

Next, Paré dropped a toad—regarded as a highly poisonous creature in his day—into a bucket of water with another piece of horn, and left them to soak together for three days. Far from dying, Paré wrote, the toad at the end of that time was "as lively as when I put it in the pail."

He mentioned that great physicians of the ancient world like Hippocrates had never said anything about the medicinal value of unicorn horn. He added that experienced physicians of his time—including himself—used it in treatments only because their patients demanded it. "The world wants to be deceived," he wrote.

There was loud and immediate opposition to Paré's

views. One defender of the unicorn claimed that the animal must exist because so many people for so many centuries had believed that it did.

Paré answered the man with these words: "Mere duration of time is not enough to prove the existence and value of the unicorn. Its vogue is founded upon opinion, but the truth depends upon fact. Therefore it does no good to cite against me the popes and emperors and kings who have kept unicorn horns in their treasuries, for such men are not competent judges of natural things."

Paré ended his argument by saying, "I would rather be right entirely alone than wrong in company with all the rest of the world."

While Paré, Marini, and other sixteenth-century scholars were questioning the unicorn from a scientific standpoint, the symbolic meaning of the animal began to be questioned by the church.

At a meeting called in 1563 to reaffirm the traditional beliefs of the Roman Catholic Church, it was decreed that all "unusual portrayals" of Jesus Christ in works of art were to be avoided. After that, the unicorn was no longer used as a symbol for Jesus, and its noble image appeared much less frequently in religious art.

The unicorn lived on in nonreligious art, though — most notably in the royal arms of Great Britain.

CHAPTER TEN

Horn or Tusk?

THE UNICORN had long been featured in the coats of arms, or emblems, of medieval knights. The two had much in common. Like an ideal knight, the unicorn fought fiercely and courageously against its foes. Both showed compassion toward their fellow creatures. And the unicorn submitted willingly to an innocent maiden just as a knight devoted himself completely to the lady he loved.

Kings adopted the unicorn as their emblem also. After Robert III was crowned king of Scotland in 1390, he had two unicorns carved on the gateway to his castle, one on either side of the Scottish royal arms. According to a biographer, Robert hoped the presence of the unicorns would bring him luck and help him to be a stronger and wiser ruler. After his death, the unicorns became part of the royal arms.

Meanwhile, the lion, the king of beasts, supported the royal arms of England. It was accompanied at various times by an antelope, a greyhound, and a dragon, but when most people thought of England, they thought of a lion.

For centuries, England and Scotland engaged in a back-and-forth struggle. The English kept trying to take over their northern neighbor, while the Scots were equally determined to maintain their independence. A well-known English nursery rhyme dramatized this conflict. In it, the lion symbolizes England and the unicorn stands for Scotland.

> *The lion and the unicorn*
> *were fighting for the crown;*
> *The lion chased the unicorn*
> *all around the town.*

The actual conflict was resolved peacefully when King James VI of Scotland came to the throne of England in 1603 after the death of the childless Queen Elizabeth I. As James I, king of both England and Scotland, he replaced the dragon on the English arms with the Scottish unicorn.

The royal arms of Great Britain, as they appeared on the side of Queen Victoria's coach.

From that time on, those former enemies, the lion and the unicorn, have joined forces to support the royal arms of Great Britain.

The unicorn was put to use as a commercial symbol also. Most medicines in the seventeenth century were made and sold by druggists known as apothecaries. Sometimes apothecaries even prescribed the use of the medicines.

Since the powder from so-called unicorn horns was still being prescribed for a multitude of ailments, it was only natural that the signs of many apothecary shops in England and Europe featured carvings or paintings of a unicorn, or just of its head and horn. And when the Apothecaries' Society of London was founded in 1617, two unicorns were chosen to support its coat of arms.

However, fresh challenges to belief in the unicorn arose as more narwhal horns and skulls reached Europe and were examined by scientists. Unlike Martin Frobisher, these scientists weren't convinced the narwhal was a sea unicorn. They even questioned whether the creature's horn *was* a horn.

In an atlas published in 1621, the pioneer geographer Gerhardus Mercator wrote: "Among the fish of Iceland is included the narwhal. It has a tooth in its head which

Carved unicorn head with a narwhal tusk for a horn. It was used as a sign above a German apothecary shop.
GERMANISCHES NATIONALMUSEUM, NUREMBERG.

projects to a length of as much as ten feet. Some sell this tooth as a unicorn's horn."

The Danish physician Ole Worm enlarged on Mercator's description of the narwhal. Worm collected objects from all over the world and gathered them together in his own museum, which was a great attraction in the Danish capital, Copenhagen. On exhibit were geological specimens, stuffed animals, and a narwhal horn and partial skull.

Speaking in Copenhagen in 1638, Worm began by stating that the narwhal's horn was not a horn at all, but a tooth or tusk. Worm went on to describe the narwhal skull in his collection, and the way in which the tusk grew out of the left side of the upper jaw. He offered no explanation for the curious fact that the narwhal apparently had only one such tusk whereas most creatures with tusks, horns, or antlers had them in pairs.

Despite Worm's detailed description, many of his fellow Danes chose to keep on believing in the legend of the unicorn. King Frederick III, who ruled Denmark from 1648 to 1670, owned a vast number of "unicorn horns." From them he had the royal craftsmen build a throne that became one of the wonders of Europe. The throne's legs, arms and supporting pieces were all made of the horns.

Frederick's successor, King Christian V, was crowned in the throne in 1671. During the ceremony, the presiding bishop remarked, "History tells us of the great King Solomon that he built a throne of ivory and adorned it with pure gold. But your majesty is seated on a throne which, though like King Solomon's in the splendor of its materials and its shape, is unparalleled in any kingdom. For it is the only throne ever to be made from the horns of unicorns."

Left, the throne of "unicorn horns" that was made for King Frederick III of Denmark. Beside it is the Queen's throne.

THE ROYAL DANISH COLLECTIONS AT ROSENBORG PALACE, COPENHAGEN.

Of course the horns in the throne were really narwhal tusks, but the Danish bishop said nothing about that. Perhaps he did not know the truth, or perhaps he chose to ignore it.

Others were not so trusting. The writings of Mercator and Ole Worm had spread, and the market for unicorn horns had begun to weaken. When a Danish merchant tried to sell a large narwhal tusk to the grand duke of Moscow, claiming it was a genuine unicorn horn, the duke's physician told him it was just the tooth of a fish. Unable to prove otherwise, the merchant could do nothing but pack up the tusk and return to Denmark.

By the eighteenth century, belief in the unicorn and the miraculous powers of its horn was fading everywhere. In 1746, unicorn horn was removed from the list of effective medications in England by the same society of apothecaries that had adopted the unicorn as its emblem a hundred years earlier.

After the French Revolution and the overthrow of the king, the eating utensils of the rulers who followed were no longer made of narwhal tusks. The revolutionaries also seized the Unicorn Tapestries from their noble owners and handed them over to local peasants. For many years afterward, the tapestries were used to cover the peasants' fruit trees on frosty nights in the fall, and to protect the potatoes in their barns from freezing in winter.

Finally, the French zoologist Baron Georges Cuvier appeared to deal the unicorn a death blow when he announced in 1827 that it was probably just a fairy tale.

Cuvier backed up his charge with evidence gathered from anatomical studies he had made of goats, sheep, and other cloven-hooved creatures. The unicorn was usually portrayed as having cloven, or divided, hooves. The front of the skull bone in all such animals was divided also, Cuvier said. In order to have a single horn project from the unicorn's forehead, it would have to grow above the division in the skull. And that was simply not possible.

Consequently, wrote Cuvier, a unicorn with cloven hooves could not exist. He guessed that the unicorn ancient writers had reported seeing was either the oryx or the rhinoceros.

First Ole Worm and other scientists had produced evidence showing that the narwhal was not a sea unicorn. Now Georges Cuvier seemed to prove conclusively that no land unicorns were to be found anywhere in the world. But the noble one-horned beast still exerted a powerful hold on people. It might not exist in nature, but it lived on in the human imagination—and never more so than in our own time.

CHAPTER ELEVEN

The "Living Unicorn"

EXCEPT FOR an occasional painting, like Arthur B. Davies's dreamy *Unicorns*, no one seemed to pay much attention to the animal in the early years of the twentieth century. But then, starting in the 1930s, a great revival of interest occurred. It began in 1933 when a Maine doctor, W. Franklin Dove, turned a day-old bull calf into a unicorn.

Dr. Dove had read the writings of Cuvier, but decided the French scientist was mistaken in thinking no horn could grow above the division in an animal's skull. From studies he had made on cows, Dove had discovered that their horns were not outgrowths of their skulls, but grew

THE METROPOLITAN MUSEUM OF ART, BEQUEST OF LIZZIE P. BLISS, 1931.

Unicorns *by the American artist Arthur B. Davies (1862–1928).*

separately and then became rooted to the skulls. Thus, Dove theorized, there was no biological reason why a horn couldn't be attached to both sides of the division in the skull.

Every young animal that later grows horns has small bits of tissue called horn buds on the sides of its skull. To prove his theory, Dove performed a relatively simple operation on the bull calf. He transplanted the calf's horn buds from the sides to the middle of its skull, and arranged them so that they touched each other across the central division. As the calf matured, Dr. Dove hoped the buds would join together and grow into a single horn.

And that's exactly what happened. The horn emerged, thick and straight, and the unicorn bull seemed perfectly content with it. He used it to pass under fences by raising the bottom wire and to defend himself against other animals. But he almost never used the horn to attack another creature. Like his namesake, the unicorn—and like another famous bull, Ferdinand—Dove's unicorn bull turned out to be a gentle beast.

THE NEW YORK PUBLIC LIBRARY

Dr. Dove's unicorn bull.

Actually, Dr. Dove was not the first person to manipulate an animal's horn buds in order to create a unicorn. For centuries, Dinka tribesmen in Africa performed a similar operation on large bull calves that they intended to train as leaders of their cattle herds. However, the Maine doctor was the first scientist to offer a full description of the procedure.

While Dr. Dove was busy in the 1930s creating and observing his live unicorn, the unicorn of the imagination also experienced a rebirth. It was inspired by the magnificent Unicorn Tapestries, which went on display in a New York City museum in 1938.

The tapestries had traveled a long road before reaching New York. After being used to protect fruits and potatoes from frost in the years following the French Revolution, they were discovered by their former owners, who bought them back and hung them once more in the family chateau. In 1922 the tapestries were offered for sale and John D. Rockefeller, Jr., the American millionaire, purchased them.

Entranced by their beauty, Rockefeller had a special room designed for the tapestries in his New York City town house where they covered all of the four walls. But when plans were announced for creating the Cloisters,

a museum devoted to medieval art, Rockefeller decided to donate the Unicorn Tapestries to it. As much as he loved the tapestries himself, he wanted a wider public to have an opportunity to enjoy them.

In the years since the tapestries went on display at the Cloisters, hundreds of thousands of people have passed through the gallery where they are hung. As they have stood in awe before the seven richly colored panels, an enduring image of the unicorn has become fixed in their minds. Ever afterward, when they think of the animal, the unicorn in the tapestries will probably come to mind— a noble, horselike creature with a creamy coat, a curly goatlike beard, a plumed tail, and a single long, straight horn.

It is this image that we are most familiar with today. It has spread far beyond the tapestries and is now used to decorate everything from greeting cards to posters to mugs to T-shirts. It is also the animal we most often see in the illustrations for stories about unicorns. And it served as the inspiration for another attempt, like Dr. Dove's, to create a man-made unicorn.

In 1985, the Ringling Brothers and Barnum & Bailey

Gothic doorway leading into the room at the Cloisters containing the Hunt of the Unicorn *tapestries.*

Circus announced a spectacular new attraction: The "Living Unicorn." It rode into the circus arena on a glittering gold float. Beside it stood a blond young woman dressed like a princess—or the maiden who tamed the unicorn in the old stories. As band music played, the snowy white creature waved its long single horn in time with it.

"How marvelous!" an old woman was quoted as saying.

But a little girl watching the "unicorn" perform said, "It's just a goat."

The little girl was right. It was one of four billy goats whose horn buds had been transplanted by a California couple in the same way Dr. Dove had transplanted the horn buds of the bull calf. The circus had bought all four animals, trained them, and used them alternately in performances. U.S. Department of Agriculture inspectors examined the goats and said the transplantations had probably been painless. They declared the animals were healthy and apparently happy.

But animal-rights activists were not convinced. They promised to lobby for a federal law prohibiting the public display and exploitation of beasts whose bodies had been altered. Stung by the bad publicity, the circus soon dropped the living unicorn from its roster of stars.

Meanwhile, conservationists were taking up the cause of one of the unicorn's real-life models—the rhinoceros.

PHOTOGRAPH BY ROBERT McELROY. WOODFIN CAMP & ASSOCIATES.

The "Living Unicorn" enters the ring at the Ringling Brothers and Barnum & Bailey Circus.

CHAPTER TWELVE

The Rhino, the Narwhal, and the Unicorn

IN PREHISTORIC TIMES, one- and two-horned rhinos roamed across all the continents, but by the twentieth century only five species were left. These included the black rhinos and white rhinos of Africa, which have two horns, and the single-horned species of India, Sumatra, and Java.

In 1968, there were an estimated 65,000 black rhinos in Africa, but by 1989 the population had shrunk to about 3,500. The one-horned Indian rhino could formerly be found throughout the vast Indian subcontinent. By the late 1980s only 600 of the animals were alive in remote regions of northern Bengal, Nepal, and Assam.

Why has the rhino population declined so dramatically? It's largely due to illegal hunting by poachers. Since ancient times the rhino's horn—like the unicorn's—has been thought to possess wondrous medicinal powers. Today, Asian pharmacists in rural areas still prescribe powdered rhino horn as a treatment for snakebite, typhoid fever, headaches, and even insanity. As a result, poachers can obtain high prices for the horns. One that is in good condition and fairly large brings anywhere from $5,000 to $15,000 in the retail markets of Asia.

To counteract the widespread poaching, conservationists are taking various steps to protect the remaining rhinos. In Nepal, the one-horned Indian rhino—whose scientific name is *Rhinoceros unicornis*—now lives mainly in a nature preserve, the Royal Chitawan National Park. There its population grew from only about 250 animals in 1975 to between 350 and 370 in 1986.

However, poachers still managed to get into the park occasionally, slaughter several rhinos, and remove their valuable horns. So conservationists devised a new plan to help ensure the animals' survival. Working in teams, they rounded up a number of rhinos, tranquilized them, and transported them by truck to an even more remote nature reserve in the foothills of the Himalaya Mountains.

On this reserve, far from any human habitation, they believed it would be easier to keep poachers away from the rhinos.

No one knows if such measures will be successful in the face of a continuing demand for the rhinos' horns. Should they fail, the one-horned Indian rhinoceros may become extinct along with the other four species. If that happens, the rhinoceros will live on only in legend, like the unicorn it helped to inspire.

Life-size model of a one-horned Indian rhinoceros.
AMERICAN MUSEUM OF NATURAL HISTORY.

Scientists today are also trying to learn more about the other creature that contributed to the unicorn legend—the narwhal. But it remains almost as much of a mystery as when Martin Frobisher found the dead body of one on the icy shores of Baffin Island.

One reason so little is known about the narwhal is that none has lived for long in captivity. Six of them were brought back from the far north of Canada in 1970 and put on display in an aquarium in Vancouver, but all died of pneumonia within a few months. The fate of these and other captured narwhals seems oddly similar to that of the unicorn. Like them, the unicorn was often described by ancient and medieval writers as an animal that could never be taken alive.

What knowledge we have of the narwhal comes from fishermen, scientists, and others who have observed the creature in its Arctic habitat. Narwhals are not fish but air-breathing mammals like dolphins and whales. They are usually seen in small groups of two to eight, often of the same sex and age. During spring migration, herds of 300 or more narwhals have been spotted swimming north together.

It is thought—although not definitely known—that female narwhals breed in April and give birth to a single five-foot-long, 170-pound calf fourteen months later. Scientists believe female narwhals reach sexual maturity when they are between four and seven years old, and males when they are between eight and nine. By then, the males' tusks have attained their full length.

Both male and female narwhals have potential tusks in the form of two teeth in their upper jaws, one on each side. In most instances, only one of these teeth grows into a spiraled tusk, and this usually happens only in the males. Occasionally a female narwhal with a tusk is found, but such animals are rare. Even rarer are males or females with tusks on both sides of their jaws.

No one knows for sure what purpose the narwhal's tusk serves. Some scientists think the animal may spear small fish with it or use it to defend itself or to attack its enemies. Other scientists believe the narwhal may smash through thin ice from below with the tusk in order to create breathing holes. No narwhal has been seen doing any of these things, however. A more likely explanation is that the tusk is simply an indication of an adult male narwhal's sexuality, like a beard in humans.

No one knows exactly how many narwhals there are today, either. It is estimated that somewhere between 20,000 and 25,000 of the mysterious animals live in the Greenland Sea and the far northern waters of Canada.

Because the narwhal population can only be estimated,

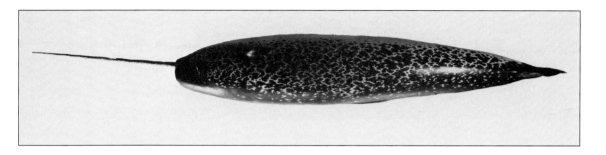

AMERICAN MUSEUM OF NATURAL HISTORY.

Model of an adult narwhal.

AMERICAN MUSEUM OF NATURAL HISTORY.

Eskimo stone sculpture of a narwhal. The tusk and fins are carved from walrus ivory.

it's unclear whether the animal faces a serious conservation problem. Narwhal tusks are still prized for their ivory and as trophies, even though no one any longer believes they're unicorn horns. In recent years, Eskimo hunters have reported annual kills of about 1,000 narwhals, but the total is undoubtedly higher.

If we're ever to know more about the elusive narwhal, we'll have to find a way to capture some live animals and maintain them for observation and study. In the meantime, we can only guess whether the "sea unicorn," like the rhinoceros, is in danger of extinction.

The one animal connected to the unicorn legend that seems assured of survival—at least in the human imagination—is the unicorn itself.

Other mysterious creatures have fascinated people in the twentieth century. There is Bigfoot, the furry half man–half ape that is said to live in the mountains of the Pacific Northwest. And a similar apelike creature, the Abominable Snowman, that travelers say they have sighted in the high Himalayas. And the Loch Ness monster, a dinosaur-like reptile that hundreds of people claim to have seen swimming in a deep Scottish lake. But none of these creatures exerts as strong a hold on our imaginations as the unicorn.

"The Unicorn in Captivity," the last of the tapestries in the Hunt of the Unicorn *series.*

Why should this be? We no longer think of the unicorn as a symbol of Jesus Christ. We no longer believe its horn will protect us from poisons or cure our ills. What need does the unicorn satisfy in us then?

Perhaps it is one of the most basic human needs of all: the need to believe in an ideal.

Whether the unicorn was the wild ass described by Ctesias, or the *ki-lin* of China, or the unicorn man of India, it was always portrayed as an ideal being. Never was this more true than of the animal pictured in the Unicorn Tapestries. In its actions, it displayed many of the qualities people valued most highly in the Middle Ages, and continue to value today. It was by turns gentle, considerate, strong, brave, loving, and finally, in the face of death, noble.

Modern science may tell us that no such animal as the unicorn could possibly exist. But we need to believe that its qualities do. Those qualities of strength and sensitivity, of courage and independence, inspired our ancestors and still have the power to inspire us. People in the future will probably be inspired by them, too, whenever they see the proud image of the unicorn.

Bibliography and Reading List

ALTHOUGH MANY PICTURE BOOKS and stories about unicorns have been written for young people, I found no good informational books about them during the course of my research. All the books and articles listed below were published for adults. Because of their illustrations and writing style, those marked with an asterisk (*) would probably be of the most interest to young readers.

Brooke-Little, J. P. *Royal Heraldry: Beasts and Badges of Britain.* Derby, England: Pilgrim Press Ltd., 1981.

*Bruemmer, Fred. "Arctic Treasures." Article in *Natural History,* June, 1989.

Buitenen, J.A.B., translator and editor. *The Mahabharata*. Chicago and London: University of Chicago Press, 1975.

Caesar, Julius. *The Conquest of Gaul*. Translated by S. A. Handford. Harmondsworth, England: Penguin Books, 1951.

*Clark, Kenneth. *Animals and Men*. New York: William Morrow and Company, Inc., 1977.

Daniel, Glyn. *A Short History of Archaeology*. New York: Thames and Hudson, 1981.

*Freeman, Margaret B. *The Unicorn Tapestries*. New York: The Metropolitan Museum and E. P. Dutton & Co., Inc., 1976.

*Hathaway, Nancy. *The Unicorn*. New York: Avenel Books, 1984.

Kathman, Barbara A. *A Cleveland Bestiary*. Cleveland: The Cleveland Museum of Art, 1982.

*Lopez, Barry. *Arctic Dreams: Imagination and Desire in a Northern Landscape*. New York: Charles Scribner's Sons, 1986.

McAfee, Nancy, Marjorie Williams, and John E. Schloder. *Images of the Mind*. Cleveland: The Cleveland Museum of Art, 1987.

*Mishra, Hemanta Ray, and Eric Dinerstein. "New ZIP Codes for Resident Rhinos in Nepal." Article in *Smithsonian*, September, 1987.

*Piggott, Juliet. *Japanese Mythology*, rev. ed. New York: Peter Bedrick Books, 1983.

*Reeves, Randall R., and Edward Mitchell. "The Whale Behind the Tusk." Article in *Natural History*, August, 1981.

*Schrader, J. L. *A Medieval Bestiary*. New York: The Metropolitan Museum of Art, 1986.

Shepard, Odell. *The Lore of the Unicorn*. New York: The Metropolitan Museum of Art, 1982.

Toynbee, J. M. *Animals in Roman Life and Art.* Ithaca, N.Y.: Cornell University Press, 1973.

*Vietmeyer, Noel D. "Rare Narwhals Inspired the Myth of the Unicorn." Article in *Smithsonian*, February, 1980.

*White, T. H. *The Book of Beasts.* New York: Dover Publications, Inc., 1984.

Williams, C.A.S. *Outlines of Chinese Symbolism and Art Motives.* New York: Dover Publications, Inc., 1976.

Williamson, John. *The Oak King, the Holly King, and the Unicorn.* New York: HarperCollins Publishers, 1986.

In addition, I gathered a great deal of fascinating information from two gallery talks given by Janetta Rebold Benton at the Cloisters branch of The Metropolitan Museum of Art in New York City. The first dealt with the portrayal of animals in medieval art, and the second explored the symbolic meanings to be found in the Unicorn Tapestries.

—J.C.G.

Index

Page numbers in *italics* refer to illustrations.